GRAPHIC MODERN HISTORY: WORLD WAR I

ON THE EASTERN FRONT

By Gary Jeffrey & Illustrated by Nick Spender

Crabtree Publishing Company
www.crabtreebooks.com

Crabtree Publishing Company

www.crabtreebooks.com

Created and produced by:
David West Children's Books

Project development, design, and concept:
David West Children's Books

Author and designer: Gary Jeffrey

Illustrator: Nick Spender

Editor: Lynn Peppas

Proofreader: Kelly McNiven

Project coordinator: Kathy Middleton

Print and production coordinator:
Katherine Berti

Prepress technician: Katherine Berti

Photographs: p7m, Garitan, p45m,b,
Bundesarchiv

Library and Archives Canada Cataloguing in Publication

Jeffrey, Gary
On the Eastern Front / Gary Jeffrey ; illustrated by
Nick Spender.

(Graphic modern history : World War I)
Includes index.
Issued also in electronic formats.
ISBN 978-0-7787-0910-7 (bound).
--ISBN 978-0-7787-0916-9 (pbk.)

1. World War, 1914-1918--Campaigns--Eastern Front--
Juvenile literature. 2. World War, 1914-1918--Campaigns--
Eastern Front--Comic books, strips, etc. 3. Graphic novels. I.
Riley, Terry II. Title. III. Series: Jeffrey, Gary. Graphic modern
history. World War I.

D551.J35 2013   j940.4'147   C2013-901120-X

Library of Congress Cataloging-in-Publication Data

Jeffrey, Gary.
On the Eastern Front / Gary Jeffrey & illustrated by Nick
Spender.
    pages cm. -- (Graphic modern history: World War I)
Includes index.
ISBN 978-0-7787-0910-7 (reinforced library binding)
-- ISBN 978-0-7787-0916-9 (pbk.) -- ISBN 978-1-4271-9253-0
(electronic pdf) -- ISBN 978-1-4271-9177-9 (electronic html)
1. World War, 1914-1918--Campaigns--Eastern Front--Comic
books, strips, etc. 2. World War, 1914-1918--Campaigns--Eastern
Front--Juvenile literature. 3. Graphic novels. I. Spender, Nik,
illustrator. II. Title.

D551.J44 2013
940.4--dc23

2013005628

Crabtree Publishing Company

www.crabtreebooks.com   1-800-387-7650

Printed in the U.S.A./042013/SX20130306

Copyright © **2013 CRABTREE PUBLISHING COMPANY**. All rights reserved. No part of this publication may be
reproduced, stored in a retrieval system or be transmitted in any form or by any means, electronic, mechanical, photocopying,
recording, or otherwise, without the prior written permission of Crabtree Publishing Company.

Published in Canada
Crabtree Publishing
616 Welland Ave.
St. Catharines, Ontario
L2M 5V6

Published in the United States
Crabtree Publishing
PMB 59051
350 Fifth Avenue, 59th Floor
New York, New York 10118

Published in the United Kingdom
Crabtree Publishing
Maritime House
Basin Road North, Hove
BN41 1WR

Published in Australia
Crabtree Publishing
3 Charles Street
Coburg North
VIC 3058

CONTENTS

FRONTIER BATTLES

On June 28, 1914, Serbian backed terrorists killed the heir to the Austro-Hungarian Empire, Franz Ferdinand. Ferdinand's assassination pulled Russia into an unavoidable war with Germany.

In mid-1914, the Eastern Front bulged west around Warsaw before dropping to trace the border of Austria-Hungary in East Galicia.

WAR NOW

Backed by its ally, Germany, Austria-Hungary declared war on Serbia. Russia, who backed Serbia, began mobilizing on July 31, 1914. This

The Kaiser was determined to beat France first, and then rush troops eastward to face Russia.

was exactly what the Germans wanted. France had been helping to rearm Russia since 1905, after it lost a disastrous war against the Japanese. Russia was underdeveloped; Germany had better troops and equipment, and a superior railway network, but it calculated that by 1917 Russia would be too powerful to beat.

It was now or never to fight a rival that had two and a half times the population of Germany, and a vast potential of raw materials. While the bulk of German troops were sent west, a lone army stationed in East Prussia guarded against any early attack.

The Imperial army was called "The Russian steamroller."

EAST PRUSSIA SAVED

As they cut through Belgium, the Germans were counting on slow Russian mobilization. Shockingly, as early as August 17, two Russian armies invaded East Prussia—the capital, Konisberg, was their target.

The Germans engaged with heavy losses. A retreat behind the Vistula River threatened. New commanders were sent and at the Battle of Tannenberg (see page 8), the southernmost army was defeated. Another battle at the Masurian Lakes (September 9–14, 1914) saw the northernmost Russian army pushed back behind the border.

Russian prisoners captured during Tannenberg. Unprepared for war, the Russians had rushed into East Prussia to help the French by drawing German troops away from the Western Front. Arguably, they helped to save Paris.

Austria-Hungary's commander was the over-ambitious Conrad von Hötzendorf.

EAST GALICIA LOST

The Russians did better against Austria-Hungary, well before tactical errors by von Hotzendorf led to the fall of the capital, Lemberg (Lviv), in mid-September. The mainly Austrian armies lost much equipment and manpower as they were thrust back against the Carpathian mountains by the generalship of, among others, Aleksei Brusilov.

Central Powers troops finally halted the Russian advance in the Carpathian Mountains in December 1914.

PULL AND PUSH

By the end of 1914, nearly 200,000 Russian soldiers had been killed, wounded, or captured in battle. Still, they had the Austro-Hungarians in a vice, and had inflicted serious losses on the German army.

With the war on the Western Front stalled, German chief of staff, Eric von Falkenhayn, sent troops for fresh offensives in the east.

CONCENTRATION OF FORCE

The idea for an attack on Gorlice, in the far south of Galicia, was von Hotzendorf's. Austro-Hungarian morale was collapsing and if the Germans did nothing, the dual monarchy might sue for a separate peace with Russia.

Italy was also threatening to join the war against her old enemy, Austria. A great victory against Russia might discourage her. On May 2, 1915, a huge artillery bombardment blasted away three corps of the Russian third army at Gorlice, creating a huge gap. Austrian and German troops poured through. The entire southern Russian line was now in peril.

German infantry at Gorlice

German cavalry entering Warsaw, the prized capital city of Poland in Russian territory, on August 5, 1915

THE GREAT RETREAT

As the offensive progressed, the Russian armies to the north pulled back to protect their exposed left flanks. The Germans ordered an attack across the whole line—a chance to encircle and destroy the entire Russian force in one go.

Stavka, the Russian high command, had no choice. Plagued by shortages of food, equipment and, most crucially, shells, they ordered a general pullback deep into Russia.

On August 21, 1915, Tsar Nicholas II dismissed his chief of staff and headed the army himself. From now on, he would be personally identified with any further military setbacks.

A GREAT FIGHTBACK

From February 1916, the French army were being bled dry by a massive German siege at Verdun, on the Western Front. They begged the Russians to launch an offensive to pull German troops away from the battle. The vigorous general, Aleksei Brusilov, had a plan.

Brusilov saw where Russian tactics had failed. Instead of a general advance, he wanted to attack in several places at once on his southwest front. This would stop the Austro-Hungarians from deploying their reserves effectively. His men would also build their trenches much closer to the German lines. Artillery would be masked. Shock troops would target weak points in the line—surprise was the essence of the plan.

Beginning on June 4, the Brusilov Offensive achieved spectacular results. In three months, it advanced around 30 miles (48 km) a day, and took over 400,000 prisoners. Austria-Hungary looked beaten. Russia rejoiced.

THE FIZZLE

Brusilov was a great general, but the others, who were supposed to launch their own offensives in support, kept to the old, losing ways. The follow-up was mismanaged. Brusilov was halted at the Carpathians as his advance fizzled out.

Brusilov's methods were noted by the Germans, who used them in their Spring Offensive in 1918. He had changed the face of war. His attack was to be the high point of the Russian army's efforts in World War I.

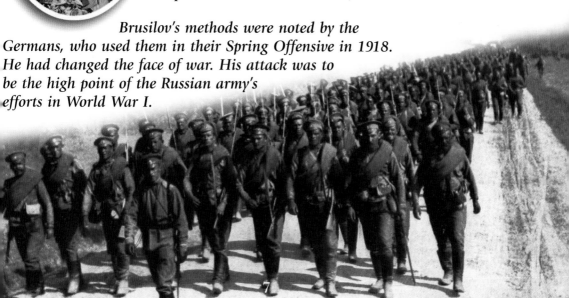

ENCIRCLEMENT
—THE BATTLE OF TANNENBERG

AUGUST 23, 1914, EIGHTH GERMAN ARMY HEADQUARTERS, MARIENBURG, EAST PRUSSIA.

AS HE AWAITED THE ARRIVAL OF THE NEW COMMANDERS, DEPUTY CHIEF OF STAFF COLONEL MAX HOFFMANN CONSIDERED THE SITUATION...

SO, OUR FIRST FIGHT BACK AGAINST THE RUSSIAN INVADERS HAS **FAILED**...

THE NEW COMMANDERS WERE HINDENBERG AND HIS DEPUTY, LUDENDORFF.

...WE FIND OURSELVES HALTED IN A LINE, SOUTH OF KONISBERG, FACING THE FIRST RUSSIAN ARMY OF RENNENKAMPF, WHO HAVE **STOPPED**...

...TO THE SOUTH, THE SECOND RUSSIAN ARMY OF SAMSONOV IS ADVANCING, PREPARING TO SWEEP UPWARDS AND...

AH, HOFFMANN! GOOD TO SEE YOU!

HOFFMANN AND LUDENDORFF HAD KNOWN EACH OTHER SINCE BEFORE THE WAR.

LUDENDORFF LED THE DISCUSSION ON STRATEGY...

ON THE WAY OVER, WE DISCUSSED OUR IDEAS, BUT FIRST I WOULD LIKE TO HEAR *YOUR* OPINION, HOFFMANN.

IT'S OBVIOUS. WE NEED TO REPEL SAMSONOV. FIRST CORPS IS ALREADY MOVING TOWARD HIM.

AND I SUGGEST ADDING TWENTIETH CORPS, AND THIRD RESERVE DIVISION.

THAT'S THE BULK OF OUR TROOPS.

AND IF RENNENKAMPF *ADVANCES?*

I BELIEVE HE WILL NOT, SIR.

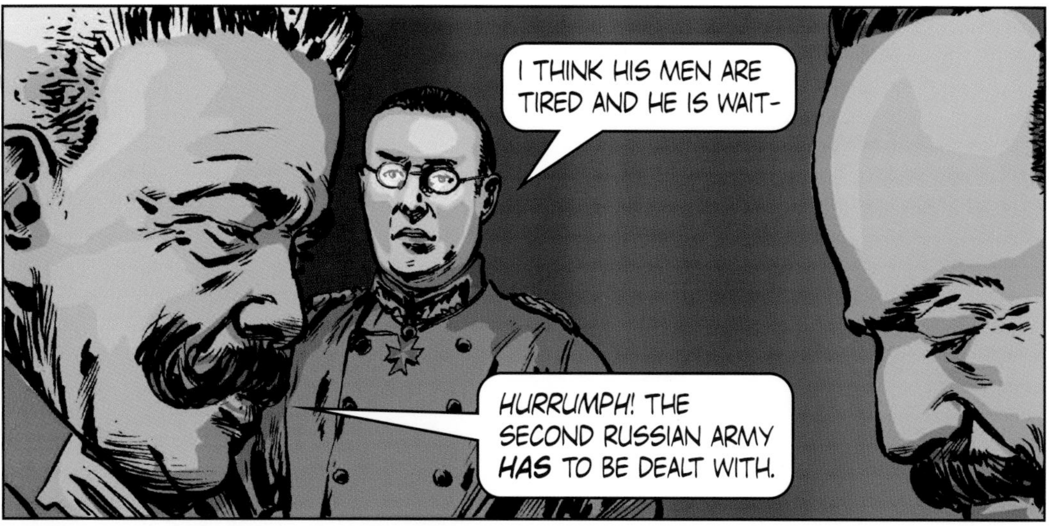

I THINK HIS MEN ARE TIRED AND HE IS WAIT-
HURRUMPH! THE SECOND RUSSIAN ARMY HAS TO BE DEALT WITH.

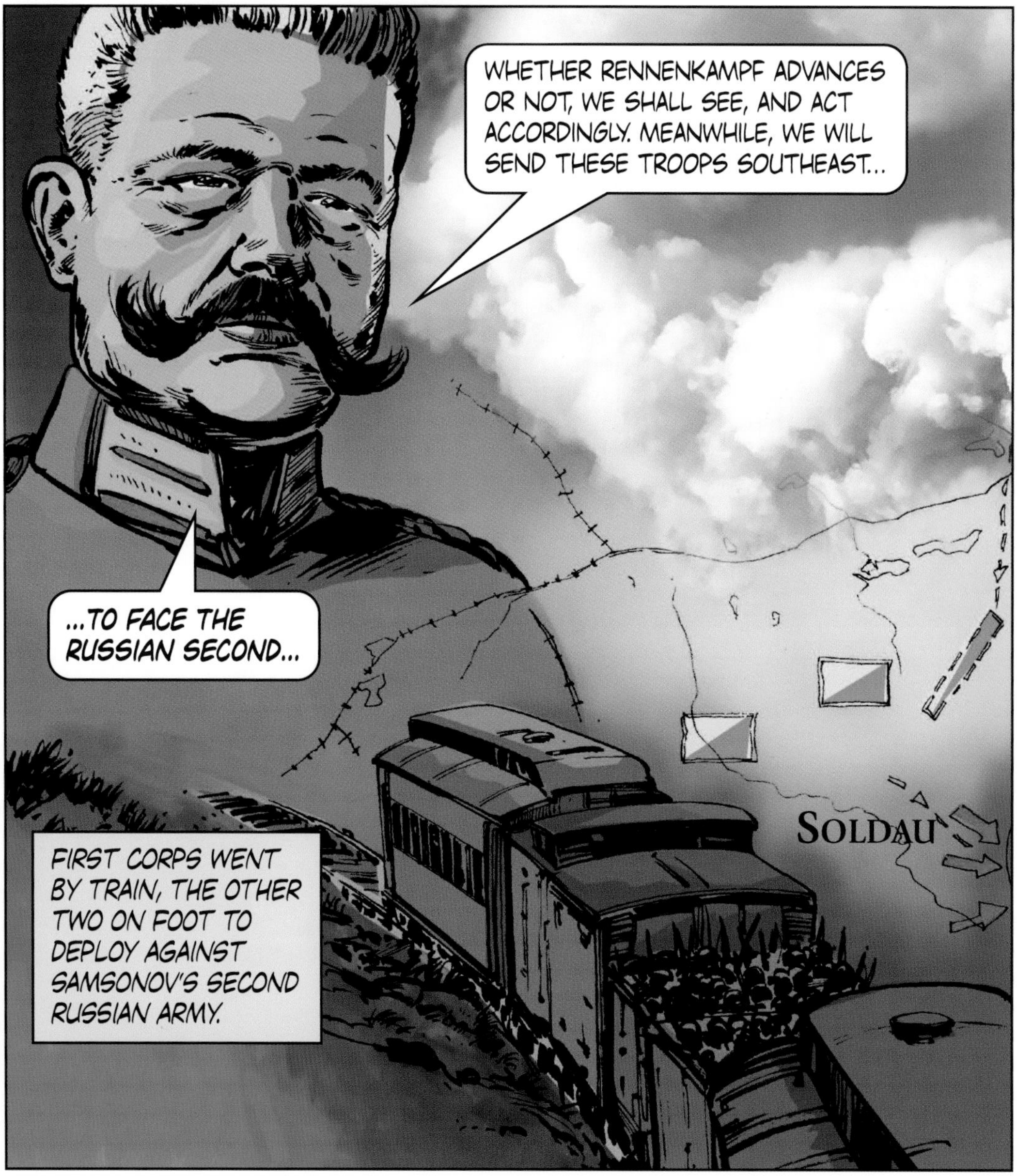

WHETHER RENNENKAMPF ADVANCES OR NOT, WE SHALL SEE, AND ACT ACCORDINGLY. MEANWHILE, WE WILL SEND THESE TROOPS SOUTHEAST...
...TO FACE THE RUSSIAN SECOND...
SOLDAU
FIRST CORPS WENT BY TRAIN, THE OTHER TWO ON FOOT TO DEPLOY AGAINST SAMSONOV'S SECOND RUSSIAN ARMY.

ON AUGUST 24, HOFFMANN AND LUDENDORFF TRAVELED TO FIRST CORPS TO SORT OUT A PROBLEM WITH THE COMMANDER.

THIS PLAN OF YOURS IS VERY **RISKY**.

HOW CAN YOU BE SURE RENNENKAMPF WON'T TURN SOUTHWEST AND REINFORCE SAMSONOV?

BECAUSE THEY **DETEST** EACH OTHER.

WHEN I WAS MILITARY ADVISER TO THE JAPANESE IN O-FIVE,* I HEARD THAT THESE TWO NEARLY CAME TO BLOWS.

RENNENKAMPF REFUSED TO REINFORCE SAMSONOV AT MUKDEN. SAMSONOV PUBLICLY **BLAMED HIM** FOR HELPING TO LOSE THAT BATTLE.

*RUSSO-JAPANESE WAR OF 1904-05

SOMEHOW I CAN'T IMAGINE RENNENKAMPF RUSHING TO HELP SAMSONOV, CAN YOU?

GENERAL VON FRANCOIS WAS THE COMMANDER OF FIRST CORPS.

ALRIGHT, ALRIGHT! I'LL START THE ATTACK ON THE TWENTY-FIFTH, EVEN THOUGH MY ARTILLERY HAS NOT BEEN BROUGHT UP.

NOR BULLETS EITHER! MY MEN WILL HAVE TO CHARGE WITH BAYONETS!

LATER...

NOT USUALLY.

SIR, WE'VE INTERCEPTED A RUSSIAN MESSAGE!

DOES THAT MAN EVER FOLLOW ORDERS?

RENNENKAMPF HAS NO INTENTION OF MOVING, EXCEPT DUE WEST. IT SEEMS YOUR INSTINCTS WERE **CORRECT**, HOFFMANN.

THREE MORE DIVISIONS WERE TRAINED AND SENT TOWARD SOLDAU, WITH JUST CAVALRY LEFT IN FRONT OF KONISBERG TO KEEP WATCH.

PWHEEEEEEEEEEE

AUGUST 26TH. THE BATTLE OPENED WHEN XVIII CORPS ATTACKED.

VON FRANCOIS HAD CONTINUED DELAYING TO GET HIS ARTILLERY READY, WHICH PROVED DECISIVE ON THE 27TH.

AT GERMAN ARMY HEADQUARTERS, THE NEWS WAS PROMISING...

SIR, FRANCOIS HAS BROKEN THROUGH TO THE RUSSIAN REAR!

ORDER HIM TO **STOP** ADVANCING. WE CAN'T RISK RENNENKAMPF FINALLY COMING TO SAMSONOV'S AID!

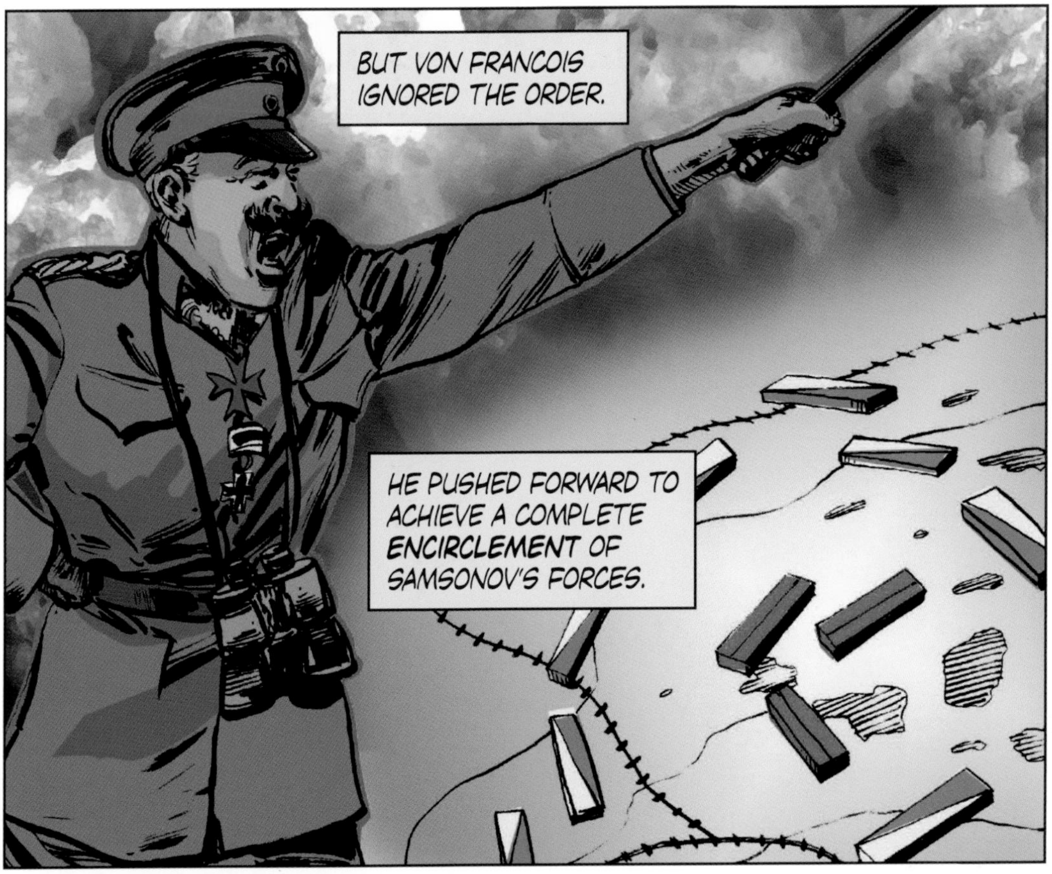
BUT VON FRANCOIS IGNORED THE ORDER.
HE PUSHED FORWARD TO ACHIEVE A COMPLETE ENCIRCLEMENT OF SAMSONOV'S FORCES.

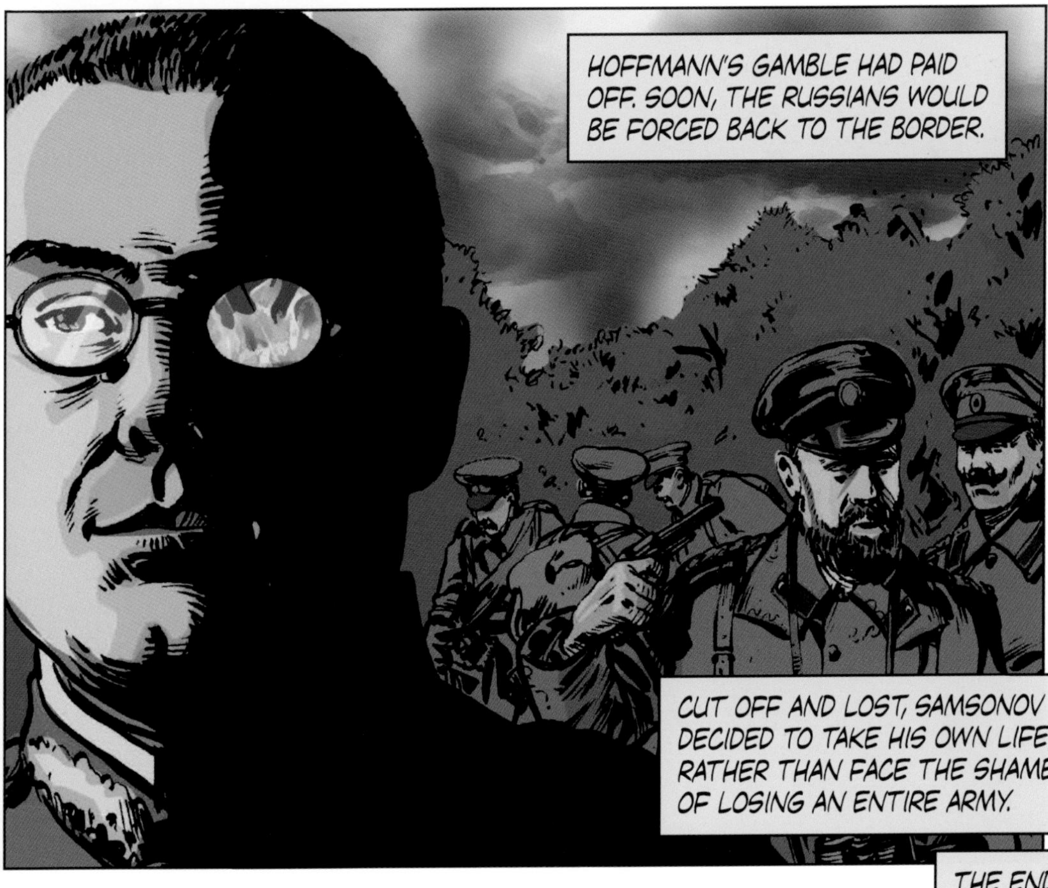
HOFFMANN'S GAMBLE HAD PAID OFF. SOON, THE RUSSIANS WOULD BE FORCED BACK TO THE BORDER.
CUT OFF AND LOST, SAMSONOV DECIDED TO TAKE HIS OWN LIFE, RATHER THAN FACE THE SHAME OF LOSING AN ENTIRE ARMY.

THE END

CAPTURED IN THE BRUSILOV OFFENSIVE

JULY 28, 1916, NEAR OFFYNA, IN EASTERN GALICIA, LIEUTENANT ERNST ENZMANN OF THE AUSTRIAN FIFTH ARMY WAS WOKEN WHEN THE WINDOW OF HIS TRENCH DUGOUT WAS BLOWN IN BY SHRAPNEL.

BLAM!

GNNNNGH!

HIS COMPANY WAS PART OF A CORPS MANNING THE FRONT LINE IN EAST GALICIA AGAINST THE RUSSIAN ADVANCE.

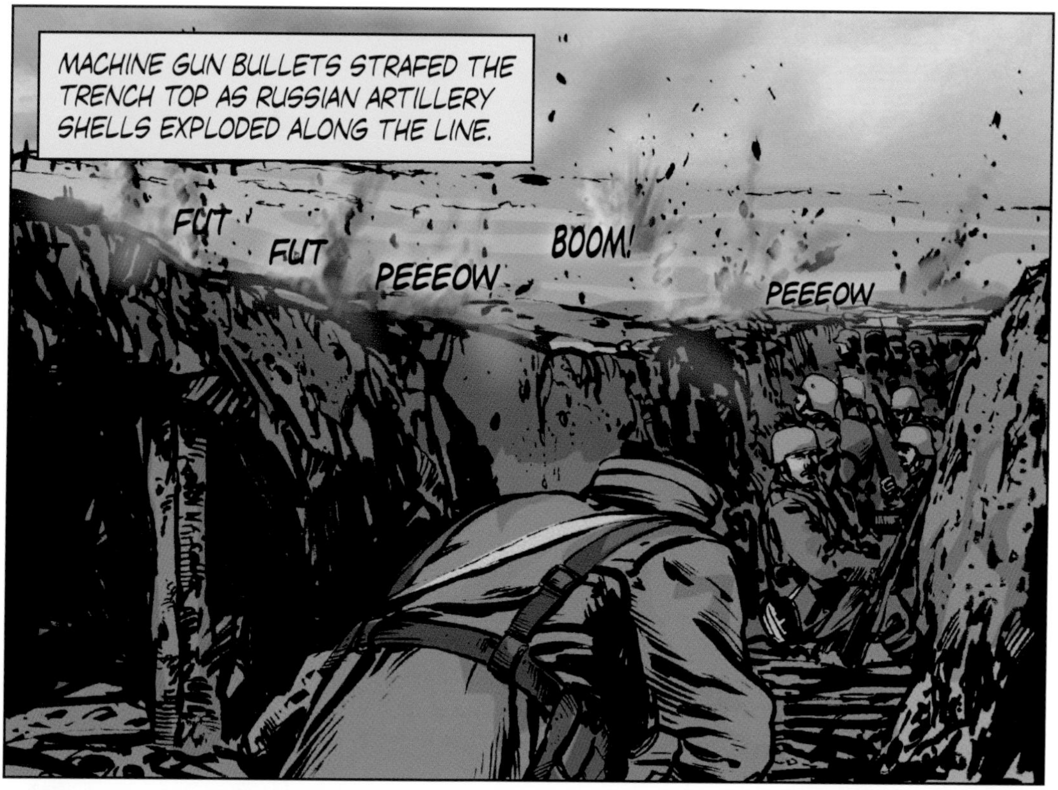
MACHINE GUN BULLETS STRAFED THE TRENCH TOP AS RUSSIAN ARTILLERY SHELLS EXPLODED ALONG THE LINE.
FUT
FUT
PEEEOW
BOOM!
PEEEOW

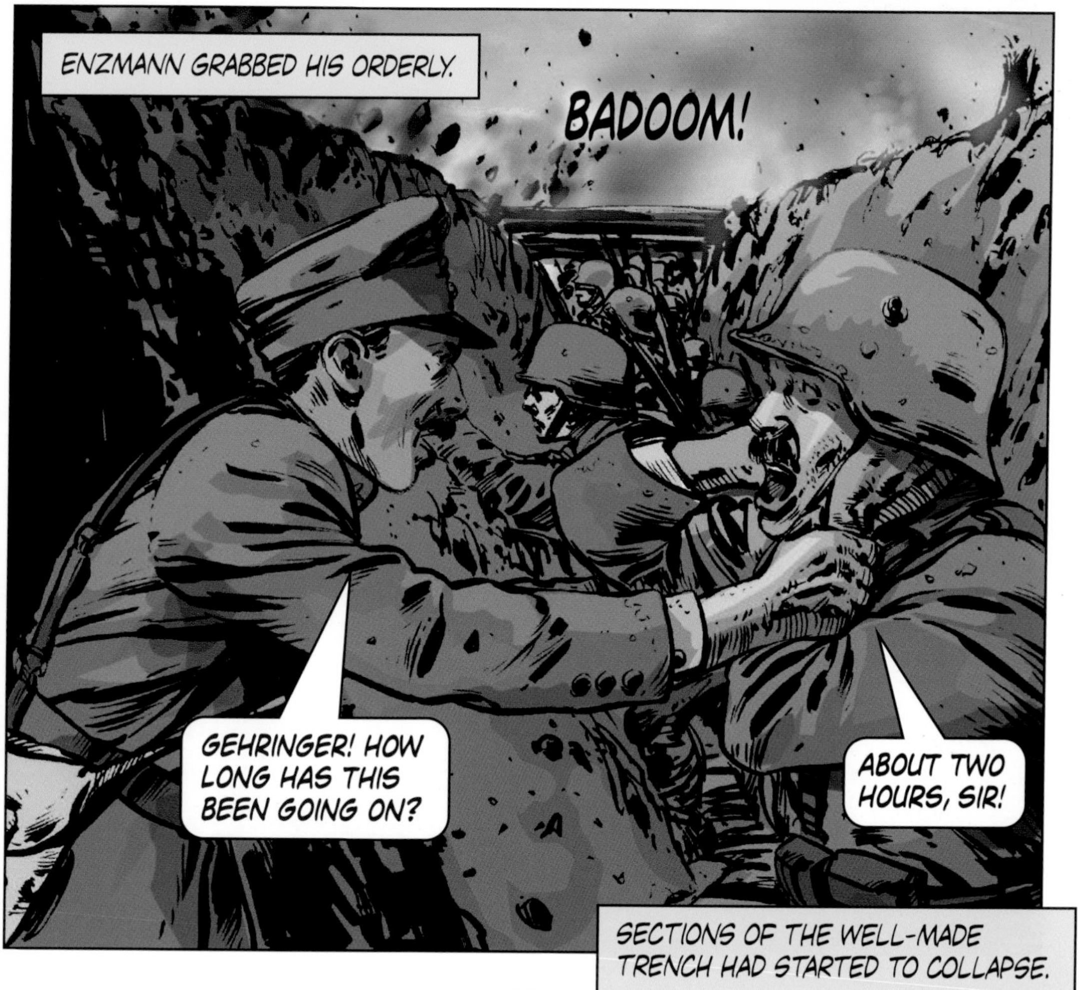
ENZMANN GRABBED HIS ORDERLY.
BADOOM!
GEHRINGER! HOW LONG HAS THIS BEEN GOING ON?
ABOUT TWO HOURS, SIR!
SECTIONS OF THE WELL-MADE TRENCH HAD STARTED TO COLLAPSE.

ENZMANN FOCUSED HIS FIELD GLASSES ON THE NEXT HILL.

THIRD COMPANY WAS TAKING A POUNDING.

BANG!

BANG!

BANG!

BANG!

BANG!

HOW CAN ANYONE REMAIN ALIVE IN *THAT*?

AT 9:00 A.M.

LOOK!

THE RUSSIANS—**THEY'RE GOING OVER THE TOP!**

ON THE HILL ABOVE THE RUSSIANS, THE SURVIVORS OF THIRD COMPANY SCRAMBLED FROM WHAT WAS LEFT OF THEIR TRENCHES.

DAT-DAT-DAT

SPOTTERS GUIDED THE RUSSIAN MACHINE GUNNER'S AIM.

THROUGH HIS GLASSES, ENZMANN WATCHED AS SUCCESSIVE WAVES OF RETREATING MEN WERE SHOT DOWN, BEFORE THEY COULD REACH COVER.

HE CONTACTED HIS COMMANDER...

ON THE HILLTOP, THE RUSSIANS WERE POURING THROUGH THE BREACH IN THE AUSTRIAN TRENCHES...

ROOOAAAR!

...DRIVING THE DEFENDERS OUT OF THEIR POSITIONS.

BANG!

AAAAGH!

COMMANDER, WE'RE BEING OVERRUN! WHAT SHOULD WE DO?

THERE **ARE** NO ORDERS. JUST HOLD YOUR LINE!

FLEEING MEN RAN DOWN THE TRENCH, PAST ENZMANN'S DUGOUT.

ENZMANN GRABBED A MAN HE RECOGNIZED.

HABERSETT, THE ORDER IS TO HOLD THE LINE!

DON'T BE A FOOL! THE RUSSIANS WILL BE ALL OVER YOU IN TEN MINUTES!

YOU CAN'T POSSIBLY HOLD OUT. I'M OFF!

CRACK! RRRRRRRR

WORKING QUICKLY, ENZMANN GRABBED MEN AND SET THEM FIRING FROM A TRENCH CORNER, INTO THE ONCOMING RUSSIANS.

FROM HERE WE CAN HOLD OUT UNTIL A COUNTERATTACK...

CRACK! RRRRRRRRRR

COMMANDER HAMANN, HELLO? HELLO?

BUT THE LINE WAS DEAD.

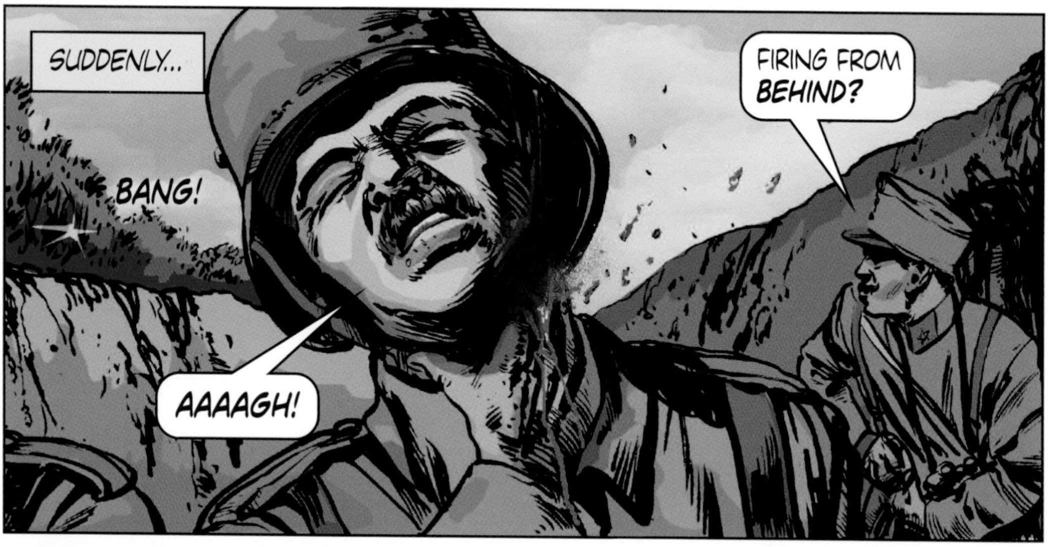
SUDDENLY...
BANG!
FIRING FROM BEHIND?
AAAAGH!

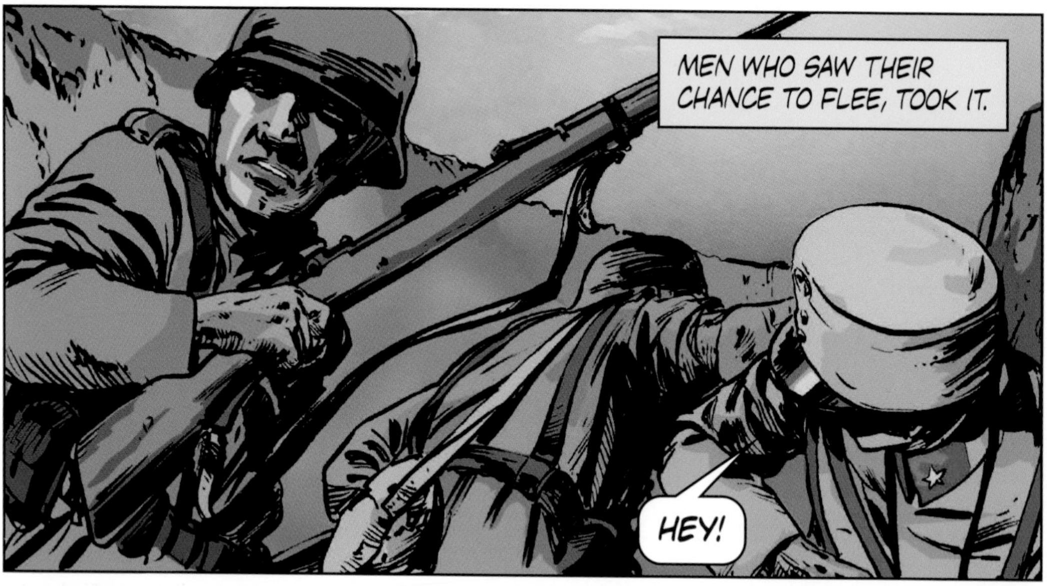
MEN WHO SAW THEIR CHANCE TO FLEE, TOOK IT.
HEY!

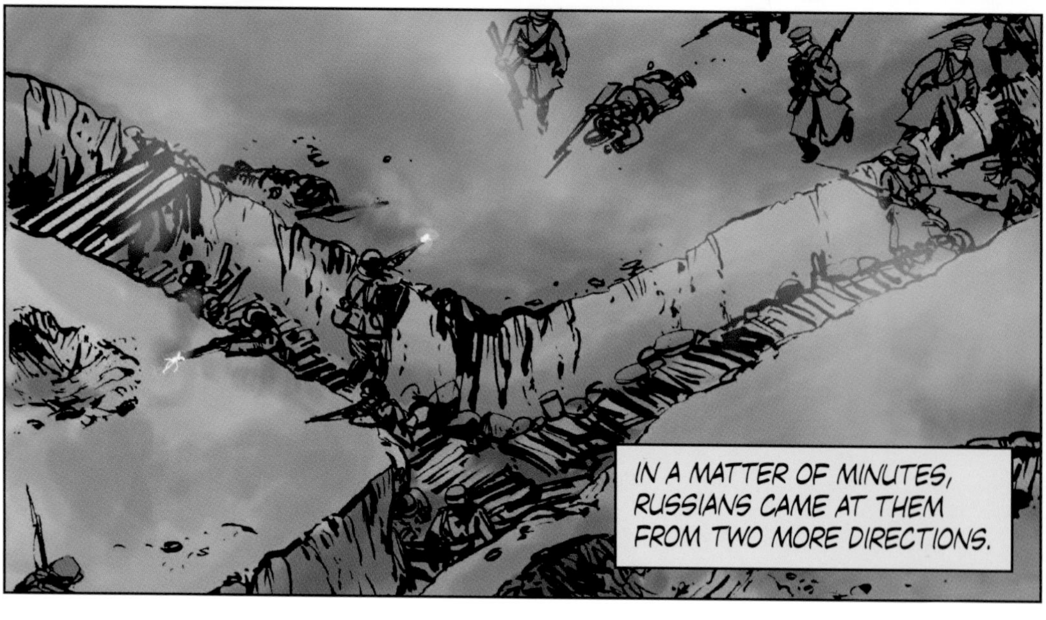
IN A MATTER OF MINUTES, RUSSIANS CAME AT THEM FROM TWO MORE DIRECTIONS.

THEY KEPT SHOOTING, BUT THE RUSSIANS KEPT COMING.

THWAP

DRRRR-DRRR

URRRGH!

ENZMANN NOW FACED A DILEMMA...

WHEN SHOULD I STOP FIRING, AND GIVE MYSELF UP?

BATTLEFIELD RULES WERE CLEAR. IF HE FIRED TO THE LAST, HE WAS LIKELY TO BE KILLED WHEN HE SURRENDERED.

NOW A BAYONET WAS COMING STRAIGHT FOR HIS CHEST.

ENZMANN SHOT AND MISSED.

BANG!

HE TURNED AND THREW AWAY HIS PISTOL.

IT WAS FAR TOO LATE. ENZMANN FELT SURE IT WAS ALL OVER FOR HIM.

HIS MOVEMENT EXPOSED HIS EXPENSIVE LEATHER CASE FOR PHOTOGRAPHIC EQUIPMENT.

THE RUSSIAN'S EYES LIT UP.

THE BAYONET WAS LOWERED.

THE RUSSIAN DROPPED HIS GUN AND GRABBED AT THE CASE.

TAKE IT! TAKE IT!

ENZMANN WAS STRIPPED OF HIS POSSESSIONS, WHILE A MACHINE GUN CREW WAS MERCILESSLY KILLED BEHIND HIM.

AAAAAGH!

OH! MACHINE GUNNERS—THEY ALWAYS GET IT.

THE RUSSIAN GESTURED TOWARD HIS LINES.

SO, WE ESCORT OURSELVES, EH?

THEN THE RUSSIANS TURNED AND CARRIED ON THEIR ADVANCE.

MAYBE WE COULD ESCAPE BACK TO OUR LINES.

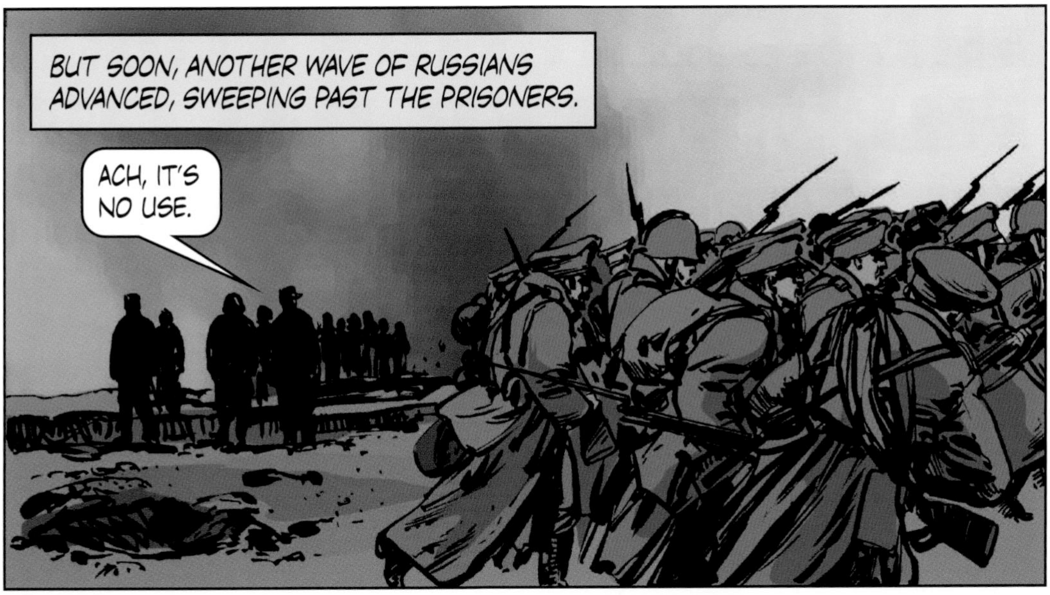
BUT SOON, ANOTHER WAVE OF RUSSIANS ADVANCED, SWEEPING PAST THE PRISONERS.
ACH, IT'S NO USE.

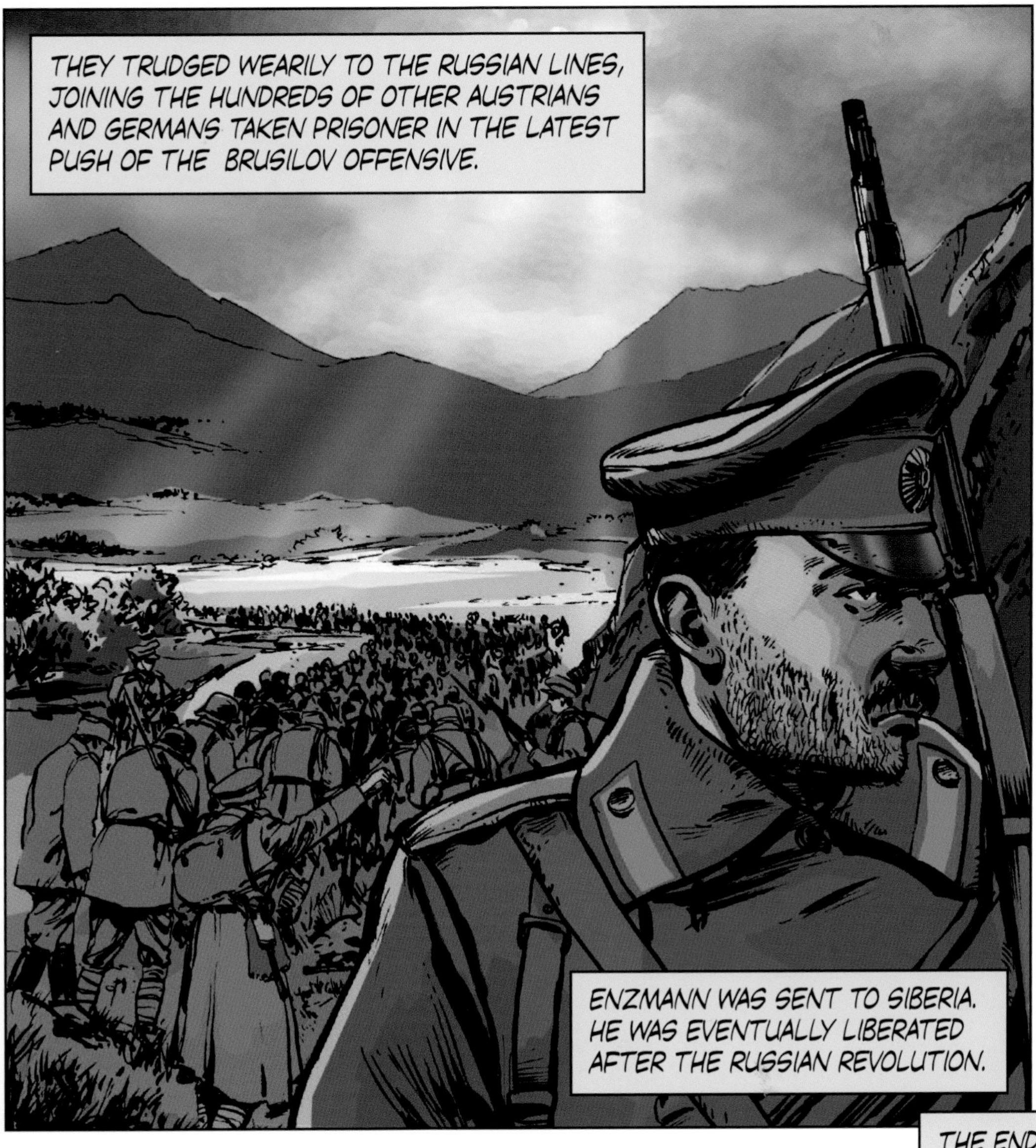
THEY TRUDGED WEARILY TO THE RUSSIAN LINES, JOINING THE HUNDREDS OF OTHER AUSTRIANS AND GERMANS TAKEN PRISONER IN THE LATEST PUSH OF THE BRUSILOV OFFENSIVE.
ENZMANN WAS SENT TO SIBERIA. HE WAS EVENTUALLY LIBERATED AFTER THE RUSSIAN REVOLUTION.

THE END

THE BOLSHEVIKS STORM THE WINTER PALACE

PETROGRAD (ST. PETERSBURG), IN RUSSIA, ON NOVEMBER 8, 1917, ABOUT 1:00 A.M.

ONWARD THEY RUSHED—THE RED GUARD, A FEW SOLDIERS, AND ONE OR TWO FOREIGN JOURNALISTS—THROUGH THE RED GATE AND INTO PALACE SQUARE.

THE DIGNITARIES OF THE PROVISIONAL GOVERNMENT HAD BEEN REFUSED ENTRY BY THE ARMY. THE PALACE WAS SPARSELY GUARDED. **THIS WAS THEIR MOMENT.**

THE CROWD PRESSED UP BEHIND THE ALEXANDER MONUMENT. THEY WANTED TO BE SURE IT WAS SAFE. AMONG THEM WAS AN AMERICAN JOURNALIST NAMED JOHN REED.

HAS ANYONE BEEN HURT?

TEN KILLED THEY SAY, BUT I DIDN'T SEE IT MYSELF.

THE LIGHTS OF THE WINTER PALACE, A SYMBOL OF THE OLD TSAR'S OPPRESSION, BECKONED.

NOW OVER THE BARRICADES.

ALL THE GOVERNMENT BUILDINGS IN PETROGRAD HAD BEEN OCCUPIED BY BOLSHEVIKS*. THIS WAS THE LAST ONE.

*RUSSIAN REVOLUTIONARIES

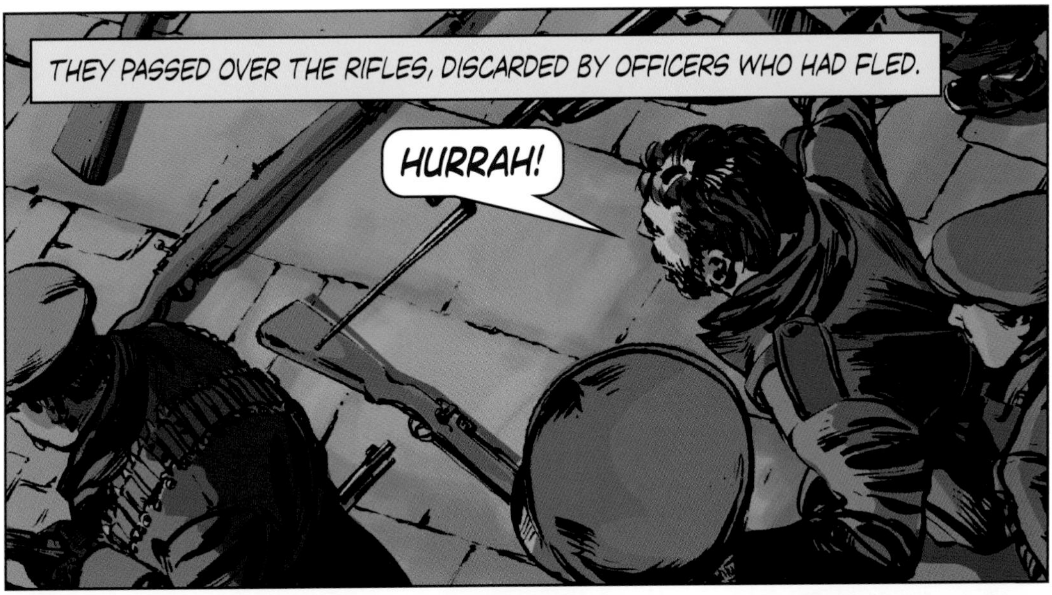
THEY PASSED OVER THE RIFLES, DISCARDED BY OFFICERS WHO HAD FLED.
HURRAH!

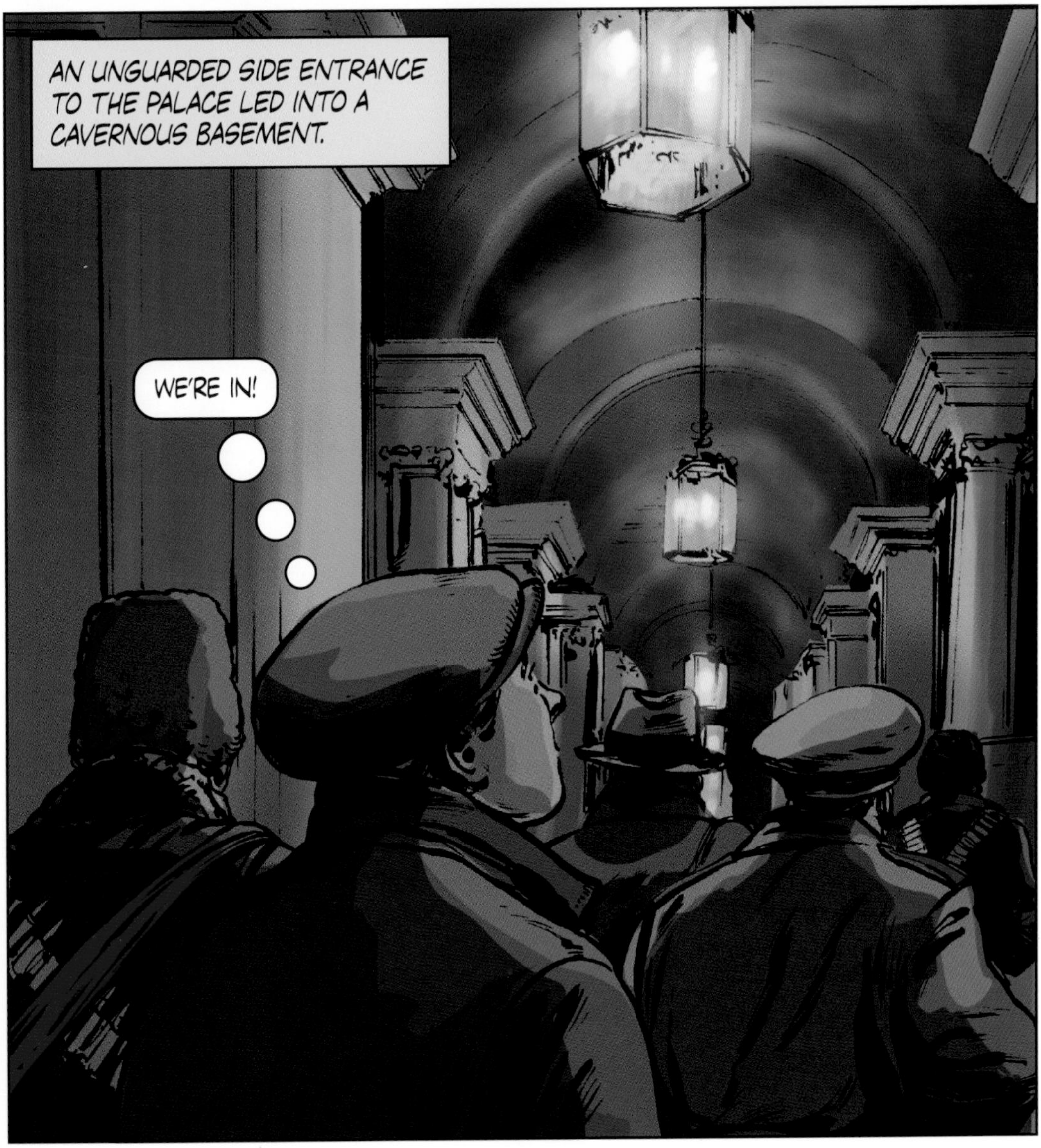
AN UNGUARDED SIDE ENTRANCE TO THE PALACE LED INTO A CAVERNOUS BASEMENT.
WE'RE IN!

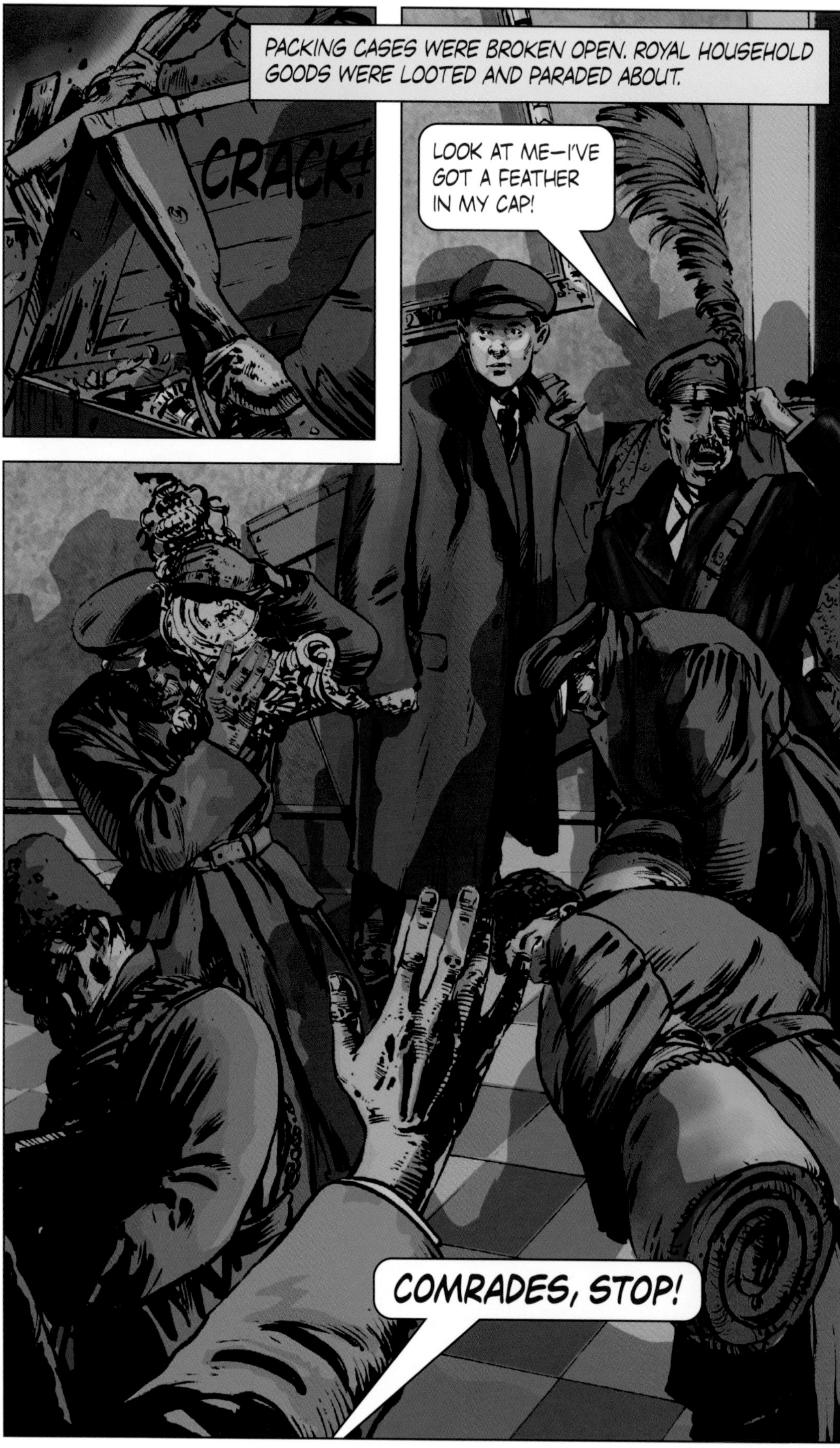
PACKING CASES WERE BROKEN OPEN. ROYAL HOUSEHOLD GOODS WERE LOOTED AND PARADED ABOUT.
CRACK!
LOOK AT ME—I'VE GOT A FEATHER IN MY CAP!
COMRADES, STOP!

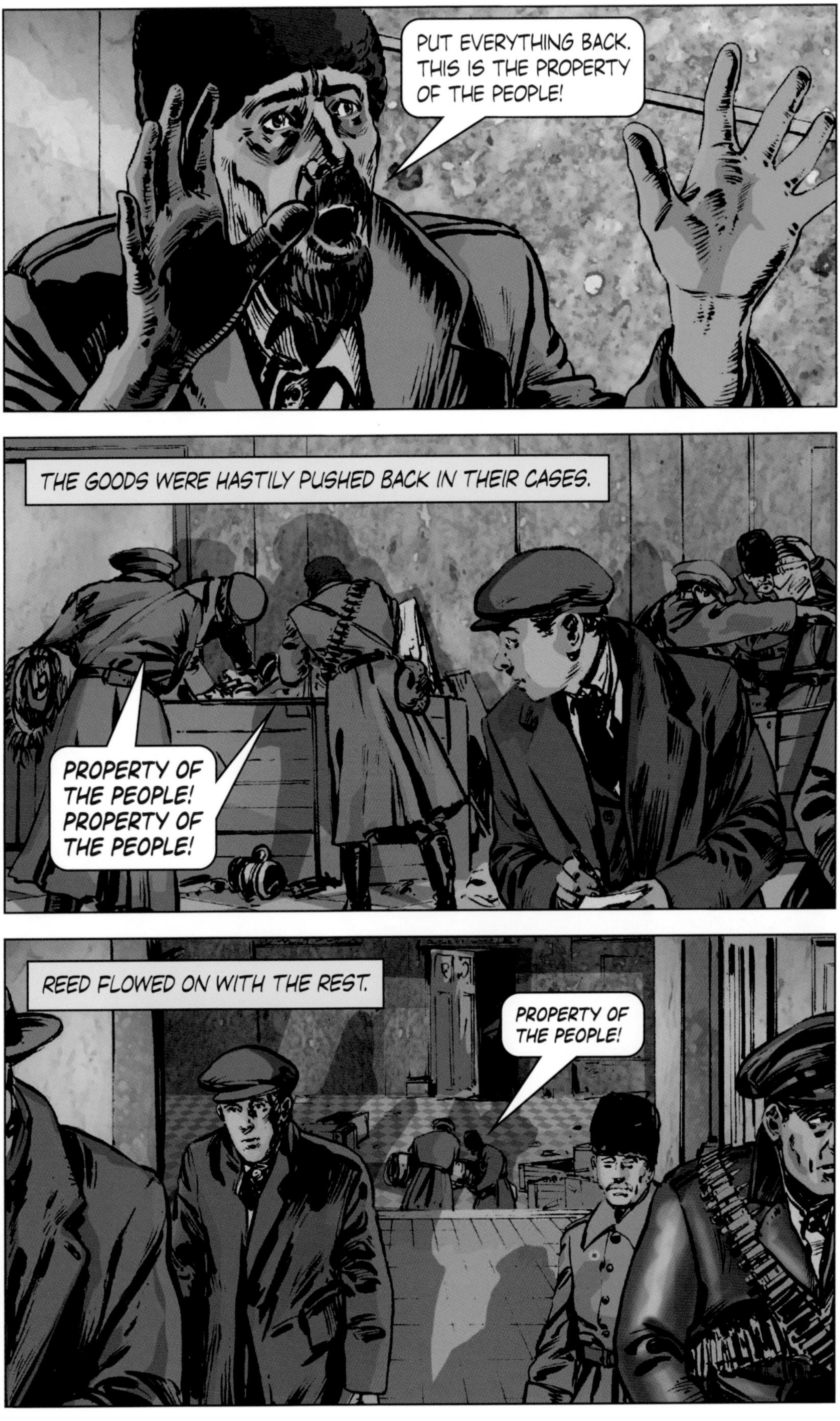
PUT EVERYTHING BACK. THIS IS THE PROPERTY OF THE PEOPLE!
THE GOODS WERE HASTILY PUSHED BACK IN THEIR CASES.
PROPERTY OF THE PEOPLE! PROPERTY OF THE PEOPLE!
REED FLOWED ON WITH THE REST.
PROPERTY OF THE PEOPLE!

IN THE WEST WING, A REVOLUTIONARY GUARD APPEARED FROM BEHIND A DOOR.

CLEAR THE PALACE!

IT'S EVERYBODY OUT, EXCEPT THE COMMISSARS*!

PEOPLE WERE SEARCHED AS THEY LEFT.

COME ON, TURN OUT YOUR POCKETS!

*A COMMUNIST PARTY OFFICIAL

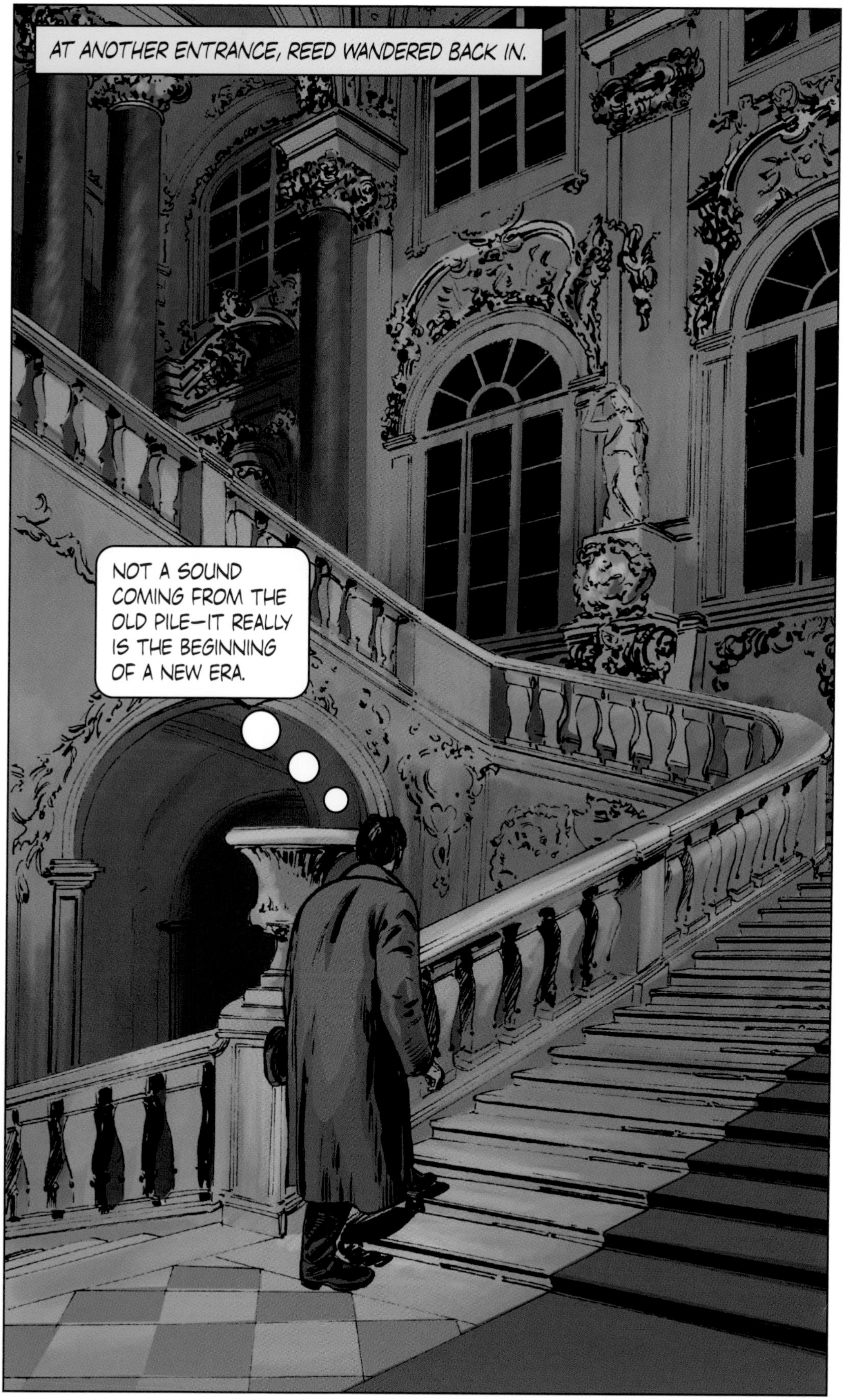
AT ANOTHER ENTRANCE, REED WANDERED BACK IN.
NOT A SOUND COMING FROM THE OLD PILE—IT REALLY IS THE BEGINNING OF A NEW ERA.

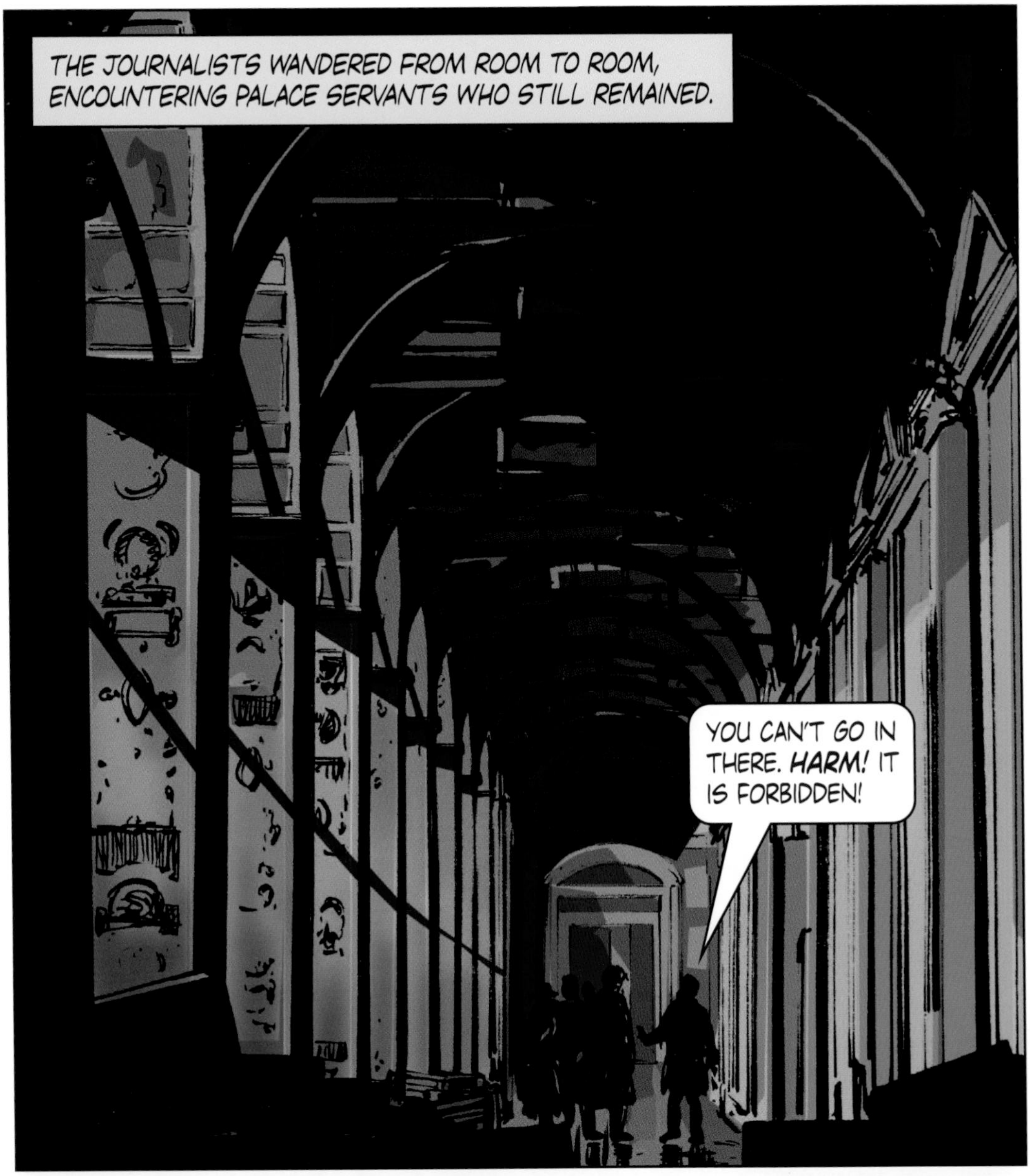
THE JOURNALISTS WANDERED FROM ROOM TO ROOM, ENCOUNTERING PALACE SERVANTS WHO STILL REMAINED.
YOU CAN'T GO IN THERE. HARM! IT IS FORBIDDEN!

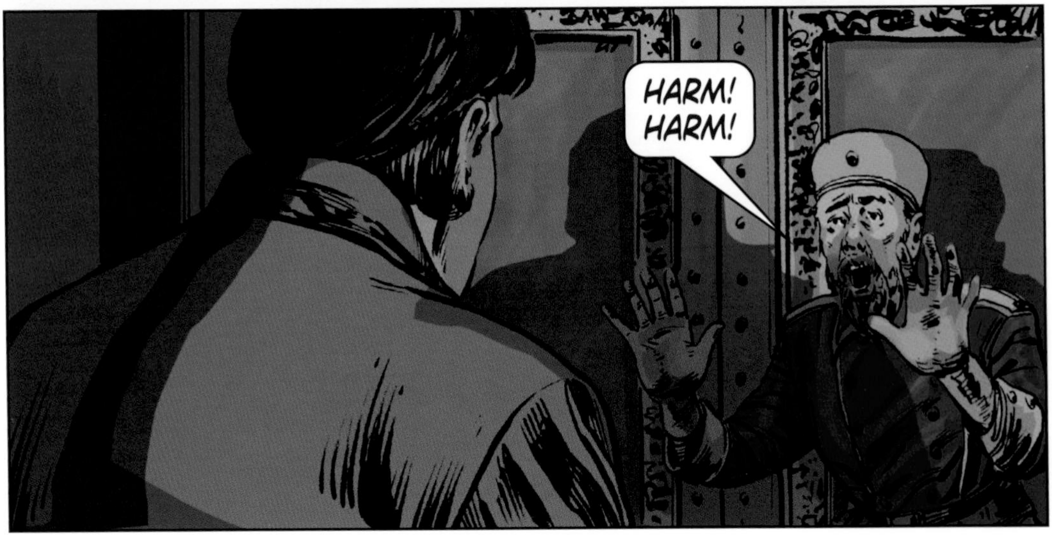
HARM! HARM!

IT WAS THE MALACHITE ROOM, SEAT OF THE PROVISIONAL GOVERNMENT THAT HAD REPLACED THE TSAR EIGHT MONTHS EARLIER.

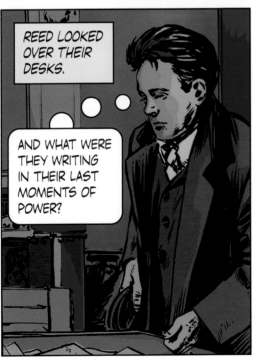

REED LOOKED OVER THEIR DESKS.

AND WHAT WERE THEY WRITING IN THEIR LAST MOMENTS OF POWER?

DOODLES?

IN THE GREAT PICTURE GALLERY, REED WAS STOPPED BY A MOB OF RED GUARDS.

WHO ARE YOU? WHAT ARE YOU DOING HERE?

TRESPASSERS!

LOOTERS!

JOURNALISTS! HERE ARE OUR **PAPERS**.

BUMAGI! PAPERS!

HE'S HOLDING THEM UPSIDE DOWN.

I DON'T THINK HE CAN READ.

PHTOOH!

REED SPOTTED AN OFFICER AS THE GUARDS CROWDED IN.

HEY, CAN YOU HELP US OUT?

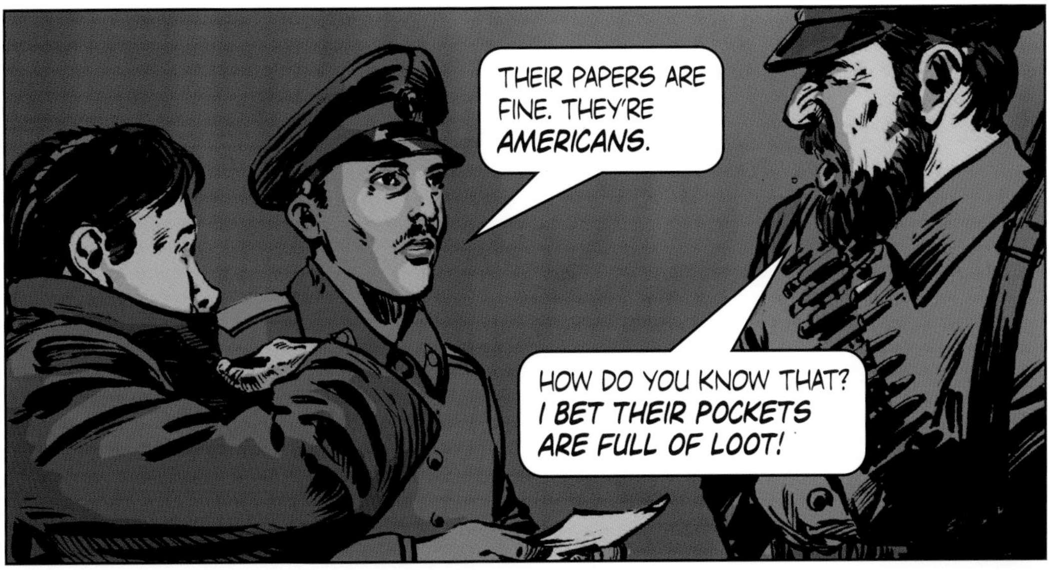
THEIR PAPERS ARE FINE. THEY'RE AMERICANS.
HOW DO YOU KNOW THAT? I BET THEIR POCKETS ARE FULL OF LOOT!

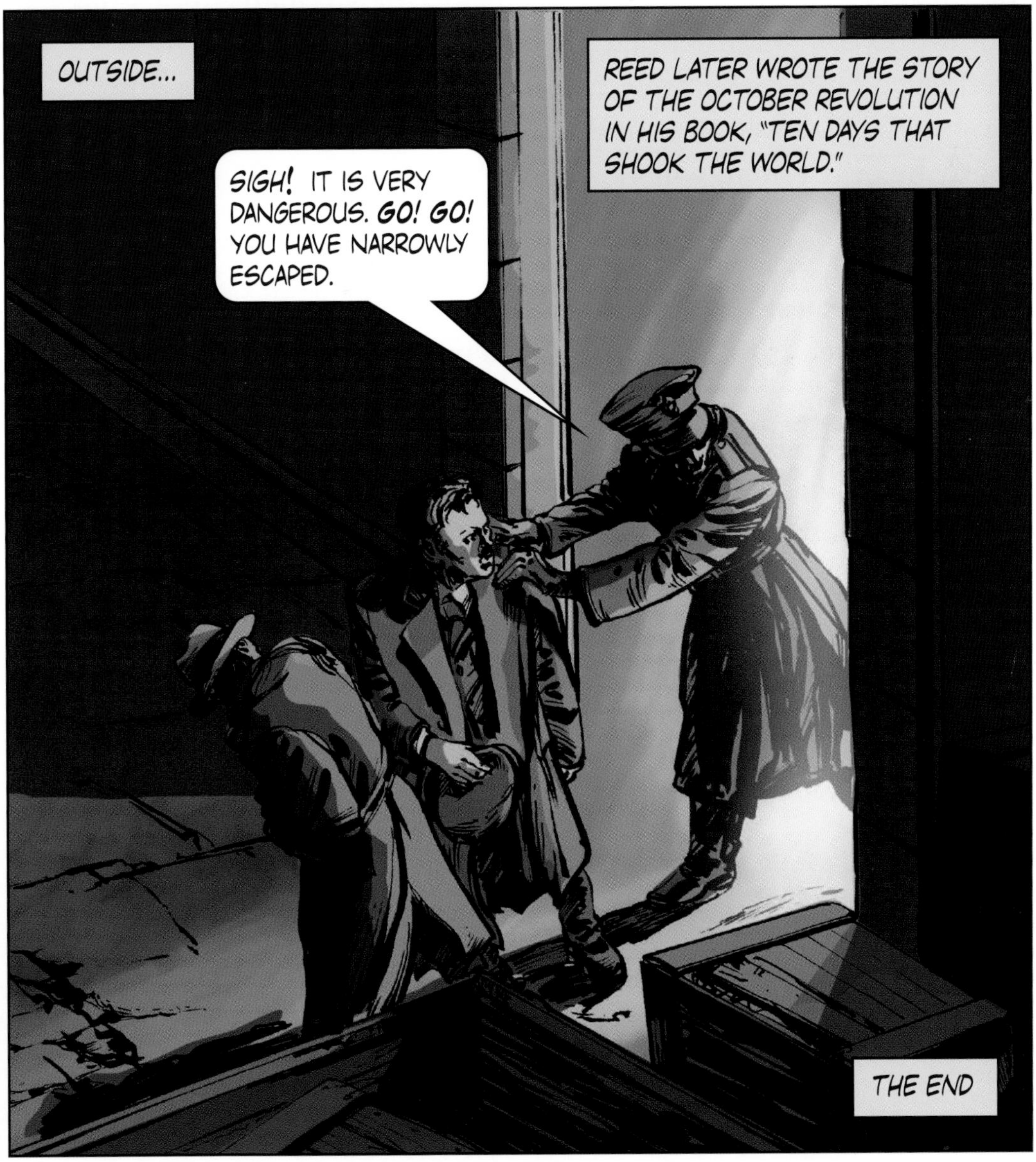
OUTSIDE...
REED LATER WROTE THE STORY OF THE OCTOBER REVOLUTION IN HIS BOOK, "TEN DAYS THAT SHOOK THE WORLD."
SIGH! IT IS VERY DANGEROUS. GO! GO! YOU HAVE NARROWLY ESCAPED.
THE END

ALL FALL DOWN

Over 1.5 million soldiers were killed during the Brusilov Offensive. Russia itself had suffered 6 million casualties since 1914 and, apart from helping its allies, nothing obvious had been gained.

Wounded Russians return from the front line

CRISIS POINT

By 1917, millions of refugees were flooding into Russia from the areas lost to the Germans. Industrial production had been stepped up, but supply problems on the overloaded railways became critical. Ordinary people began going hungry. The Tsar was away at the front and affairs were being run poorly by his German wife—who was suspected of being a spy.

OVERTHROW

Strikes and protests broke out in Petrograd in February 1917. When the Tsar ordered troops to crush the demonstrators, they mutinied.

The limited parliament (the Duma) had been dissolved. An emergency committee was running the city alongside the Petrograd Soviet (workers council). When Nicholas II arrived, he was advised to give up the throne. On March 15, he abdicated.

A protest for bread (below) on Russian Women's day in Petrograd. Fifty thousand workers also went on strike. The former Tsar, placed under house arrest (left), was now just Nicholas Romanov—an ordinary man.

Demonstrators are fired upon by troops in Petrograd, in July 1917.

REVOLUTION!

The threat of anarchy was avoided when leaders from the old Duma formed a provisional government alongside the Petrograd Soviet, led by the Bolsheviks. Soon, their powerful exiled leader, Lenin, appeared in the city. The dual power-sharing arrangement did not last for long.

Kerensky wanted to continue the war.

Lenin wanted the war to end, but struggled to organize the people against a government led by a pro-war, socialist revolutionary, Alexander Kerensky. Riots continued. Claiming Kerensky wanted help, Kornilov, commander in chief of the army, marched a force towards Petrograd. Kerensky, fearful of being overthrown, gave guns to the workers, and sent the Bolsheviks to persuade the army to withdraw. It was his big mistake. In the October Revolution the armed Bolsheviks seized power.

PEACE AND WAR

Lenin immediately declared peace with Germany. The terms were worked out in a treaty at Brest-Litovsk, in Belarus, on March 3, 1918. They were very favorable

Vladimir Lenin delivered peace...at a price.

to the Germans—who gained all of Poland, the Ukraine, Belarus, Estonia, Latvia, and Lithuania. Russia herself was about to be torn by a terrible civil war that would eventually see the rise of the Soviet Empire.

The Germans only held the territory they gained at Brest-Litovsk for eight and a half months, before they were defeated by the Allies.

45

GLOSSARY

abdicated To give up a throne, right, or power

artillery High caliber weapons used by crews during battle

assassination A murder, often of a prominent person, by surprise attack

bombardment An attack with concentrated artillery fire, or bombs

breach To break or rupture

casualties Those in hostile engagements that die, are captured, or go missing

cavalry The motorized, armored units of a military force intended for maximum mobility

cavernous Vast, deep, cave-like

deploy To arrange troops in a strategic position, ready for battle

dignitary A person who holds a high rank or office

dilemma A difficult or perplexing situation, or problem

encirclement To form a circle around, and surround

intercepted To take or seize something intended for someone else

journalist A person whose profession is to report news

liberated To be released from occupation by a foreign power

livery A distinctive uniform worn by servants, officials, members of companies, etc.

Paul von Hindenburg and other German generals masterminded a sweeping victory over Russia, but it cost them dearly in the end.

mobilization To assemble and organize armed forces for action

morale A person's emotional or mental condition with respect to confidence and cheerfulness during times of hardship

mutinied To rebel against constituted authority

offensive A carefully planned military attack

over-ambitious Too eagerly desirous of achieving success, power, wealth, or a specific goal

peril Exposure to danger, risk

plagued To be troubled, annoyed, or vexed

retreat To draw back and pull away

shortages Lacking in quantity

shrapnel Fragments from exploded ammunition

siege A military tactic that involves surrounding a place in order to capture it

superior Of higher quality

surrender To give up, abandon, yield

tactics Plan of action to bring about a specific result

trench A long, narrow hole dug in the ground to serve as a shelter from enemy fire, or attack

vigorous Energetic, active, forceful, powerful

The Imperial Russian infantry of 1916 were largely uneducated, badly trained, and poorly supplied, but magnificent in combat when used well.

INDEX